FLAVORED BUTTERS

Lucy Vaserfirer

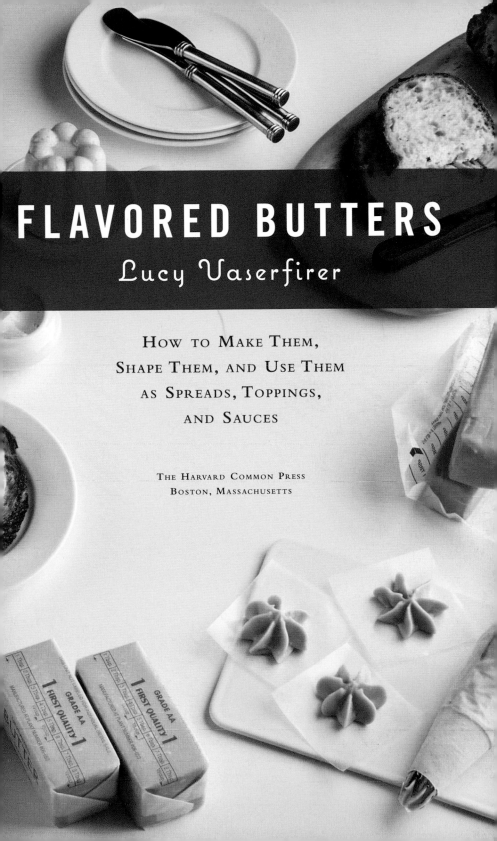

FLAVORED BUTTERS

Lucy Vaserfirer

How to Make Them,
Shape Them, and Use Them
as Spreads, Toppings,
and Sauces

THE HARVARD COMMON PRESS
BOSTON, MASSACHUSETTS

The Harvard Common Press
www.harvardcommonpress.com

Printed in China
Printed on acid-free paper

LIBRARY OF CONGRESS CATALOGING-IN-PUBLICATION DATA
Vaserfirer, Lucy.
 Flavored butters : how to make them, shape them, and use them as
spreads, toppings, and sauces / Lucy Vaserfirer.
      pages   cm
  Includes index.
  ISBN 978-1-55832-807-5
  1. Cooking (Butter) 2. Butter. 3. Cookbooks. lcgft I. Title.
  TX759.5.B87V37 2013
  641.6'72--dc23

                                                  2012035545

Special bulk-order discounts are available on this and other Harvard
Common Press books. Companies and organizations may purchase books
for premiums or resale, or may arrange a custom edition, by contacting the
Marketing Director at the address above.

Book design by Elizabeth Van Itallie
Photography, food styling, and prop styling by Lucy Vaserfirer

10 9 8 7 6 5 4 3 2 1

CONTENTS

BUTTER

Basics

$\mathcal{F}$lavored butters are culinary magic. With little more time or effort than it takes to wave a wand, memorable meals materialize! Witness these amazing transformations:

- An ordinary slab of meat turns into a gourmet grilled steak with Gorgonzola-Chive Butter (page 36) melting into it.
- A dull fish fillet becomes fit for fine dining topped with a pat of Dill, Lemon, and Garlic Butter (page 28).
- Boring steamed vegetables suddenly appear irresistible glistening with Parmigiano Butter (page 53).

This is no sleight of hand; it's true alchemy. Learn how to make flavored butter, and you'll be a wizard in the kitchen, conjuring up gourmet meals in minutes. Stash a couple of flavors in the fridge or freezer, and you'll be able to pull amazing dinners out of a hat—even on weeknights!

Flavored butters may have long been associated with fancy restaurants, but they really are so quick and easy to make. Stir together softened butter and your flavorings of choice, and there you have it. Serve a pat of your flavored butter on warm meat, fish, chicken, or vegetables; the heat transforms the butter into a rich, luscious sauce and the flavors bloom.

Flavored butter can be simple or sophisticated, savory or sweet. In its most basic form, flavored butter is nothing more than sweet cultured butter and sea salt, to be enjoyed slathered on bread. At its most luxurious, it's butter blended with black truffles or caviar. And it can be anywhere in between, with ingredients such as garlic, shallots, fresh herbs, dry spices, cheese, olives, capers, anchovies, mustard, tomatoes, citrus zest, or honey. Flavored butters are delicious served over steaks, chops, and seafood, tossed with steamed seasonal vegetables, mixed into pasta or rice, or melting on pancakes or waffles. They can be used as a spread in sandwiches and panini, on breakfast toast and evening crostini, and they can be the start of countless canapés. The variations are endless. Flavored butters can embellish any meal from a leisurely brunch to a quick weeknight dinner to an over-the-top feast.

About Butter

Real butter is the basis of all flavored butters. The flavor and texture of real butter are incomparable.

Three components—butterfat, water, and milk solids—held together in emulsion make up real unsalted butter. When butter is cold or at room temperature, the emulsion is stable, but the three components separate, or break, when butter is heated to the melting point.

Some flavor compounds are fat-soluble and some are water-soluble. Since butter contains both fat and water, it's a great vehicle for other flavors.

You'll find that you have many options to consider when you're making a flavored butter.

Unsalted butter. This has the freshest, sweetest flavor and allows the cook control over how much salt is in the final product. This is my first choice for flavored butter recipes.

Salted butter. Salt is added as a preservative and can extend the shelf life of butter considerably. This means that salted butter may taste less fresh than unsalted butter. It's also impossible to know how much salt has been added. Salted butter can be used in flavored butter recipes, but be very careful about adding additional salt.

Cultured butter. This butter is made from fermented cream and has a mildly cheese-like flavor that is desirable in some flavored butters.

European-style butter. Because of its low water content, European-style butter is slightly richer and creamier than regular unsalted butter, and it makes fine flavored butter. Sometimes cultured butters are also labeled European-style.

Goat's milk butter. The distinctive flavor of this butter is desirable in some flavored butter recipes. It's also a good alternative for those avoiding cow's milk.

SERVING SIZE

Convention says that a serving of butter is 1 tablespoon (½ ounce). So a flavored butter made with 8 tablespoons of whole butter will serve 8—unless you're generous when you portion it.

About Ingredients

Salt. Most of the recipes in this book call for coarse kosher salt, but *fleur de sel* or other coarse-grained finishing salts can be used when a little zing is desired. If you are substituting fine sea salt for coarse, use half the amount in the recipe. I find the flavor of iodized table salt harsh and offensive, and I never use it.

Pepper. Ground pepper loses potency quickly, so keep black peppercorns in a mill and grind as needed.

Some recipes call for cracked peppercorns, rather than ground, when a coarser texture is desired. A heavy mortar and pestle is the best tool for the job, but if you don't have this equipment, seal the peppercorns in a plastic bag and tap them with a rolling pin, meat mallet, or the bottom of a small, heavy pan.

Spices. Rather than buying preground cumin, coriander, mustard seed, fennel seed, cinnamon, cloves, allspice, cardamom, or star anise, buy these spices whole, then toast and grind them yourself to add a big flavor boost to your cooking. Dry heat brings out the essential oils in spices, heightening their aroma and flavor. Sesame seeds are also tastier toasted, though they are usually used whole.

The process is quick and easy. Heat a small, heavy sauté pan (not a nonstick one) over medium heat until very hot. Add whole spices and toast, stirring constantly, for 1 to 2 minutes, or until very fragrant. The spices will be a shade or two darker when they are toasted. Watch them closely so that they don't burn. Transfer to a small bowl and let cool to room temperature. Grind the spices in a mortar and pestle, a spice mill, or a coffee grinder that you use exclusively for spices.

Nuts and Seeds. As with spices, hazelnuts, almonds, pecans, walnuts, pine nuts, pistachios, sunflower seeds, pumpkin seeds, and other nuts and seeds release essential oils and get a flavor boost when toasted. While it is possible to toast them in a pan on the stovetop, using the oven results in more even browning. The one exception is sesame seeds; since they are so small, you should treat them as a spice (page 11) and toast them on the stovetop.

Spread the nuts or seeds in a single layer on a rimmed baking sheet and bake in a 400°F oven until golden brown and fragrant; they'll be a couple of shades darker when they're ready. Baking time will vary depending on the size of the particular nut or seed and whether it's whole, chopped, sliced, or slivered, so start checking after 5 minutes. Watch the nuts or seeds closely so that they don't burn, and remove them from the oven a few moments early to account for "carry-over" cooking time, since they'll continue to brown on the baking sheet even after they're out of the oven. Let them cool before use. Hazelnuts (which will take 8 to 10 minutes to toast) have a papery skin that should be removed after they are toasted. Simply wrap them in a clean kitchen towel and rub; most of the skins will slip right off.

Compound Butter

The most common form of flavored butter, usually referred to as compound butter in professional kitchens, is simply softened whole butter with flavorings mixed in. The ingredients can be just blended together or whipped until light and fluffy. The magic of a compound butter lies in the fact that it is made from whole butter and therefore has that luxurious, velvety mouth feel and rich flavor. As it slowly melts, it functions just like a fancy sauce and yet is unbelievably easy to make!

HOW SOFT IS "SOFTENED" BUTTER?

Generally speaking, when you can mix the flavorings into the butter, it's soft enough. However, for some compound butters—such as those with liquid flavorings—the butter should be very soft, almost slumping.

TOOLS AND EQUIPMENT FOR COMPOUND BUTTERS

- *Bowl and sturdy spoon.* Really, this is all you need to make the majority of compound butters.
- *Food processor.* This is useful for blending compound butters containing ingredients that must be chopped very fine.
- *Electric mixer.* A stand mixer does the best job producing whipped compound butters, but a hand mixer will do if a stand mixer is not available.
- *Microplane.* This tool is perfect for grating ingredients such as garlic, ginger, Parmigiano-Reggiano, citrus zest, and nutmeg so fine that they practically melt into the compound butter. Nobody wants to bite into a big hunk of raw garlic or a fibrous piece of ginger.
- *Parchment paper.* Parchment is ideal for forming logs of compound butter and much easier to use for the purpose than plastic wrap. Parchment paper sheets, which are available at restaurant supply stores and online, are more convenient than rolls. You can substitute waxed paper.

Making Compound Butters

Compound butters are exceedingly quick and easy to prepare. It's best to make them 20 minutes or more before you intend to serve them to allow time for the flavors to marry. But I often serve flavored butters immediately after I make them, and they're delicious. You can prepare them days in advance—or even weeks, if you freeze them.

Following the instructions in the recipe, blend together softened butter and the desired flavorings in a medium-size bowl.

INCORPORATING LIQUIDS

Small amounts of liquid flavorings, such as lemon juice and soy sauce, can be incorporated into compound butters. But the butter must be very soft and the liquid must be at room temperature to mix properly.

If the ingredients don't come together, the mixture can be heated for 2 to 3 seconds at a time in the microwave. Or wave the bowl back and forth directly over a gas burner or set it over a double boiler—again, for 2 to 3 seconds at a time—mixing vigorously as you go, until the mixture is thoroughly blended. Don't overheat the ingredients or the butter will break. You can also use an electric mixer.

Serving Compound Butters

Compound butters can be served chilled or at room temperature, depending on the desired effect. A chilled butter on a hot steak is a pleasure because the butter will take longer to melt. On the other hand, if the butter is to be enjoyed as a spread, bring it to room temperature. Refrigerated whipped butters are best softened and rewhipped before serving.

The uses for compound butters are endless. First and foremost, they make a delicious yet effortless sauce for steaks, chops, and seafood. They can be tossed with pasta or vegetables; they can be used to flavor rice, grains, and mashed potatoes; they can make baked potatoes a special-occasion dish. Dot them on fish fillets before baking or smear some under the skin of chicken before roasting. Hide a pat of butter inside a burger before you grill it. Flavored butters make popcorn pop, and they're a great topping for pancakes and waffles. They can also enrich, thicken, and balance the acidity of sauces and soups—just swirl some in right before serving.

Flavored butters are a treat slathered on bread. They're perfect in all sorts of sandwiches from panini to tea sandwiches, bringing a sweetness and richness that mayonnaise and cream cheese lack. They can be smeared on baguette slices, either before or after grilling or toasting, for bruschetta or crostini. And they can be used as spreads on canapés such as toast points, radish halves, and cucumber slices.

Last but not least, sweetened compound butters can masquerade as buttercream or frosting. There's almost nothing they can't do—compound butters make everything better!

Storing Compound Butters

Tightly wrapped compound butters will keep for several days in the refrigerator or several weeks in the freezer. Make a number of flavors and keep them on hand to add interest and variety to your cooking. Personally, I always have at least two or three different compound butter logs cut and ready to go in my freezer so that I can pull out a slice or two whenever I need it.

To do this, form a log in parchment and refrigerate it until firm. Then unwrap the log, slice it, and store the slices in a zipper-top plastic bag in the freezer.

FORMING A LOG OF BUTTER

Place the butter in the center of a sheet of parchment paper.

Bring the top of the parchment over the butter and, holding the bottom of the parchment firmly against the work surface, press into a log using a straight edge.

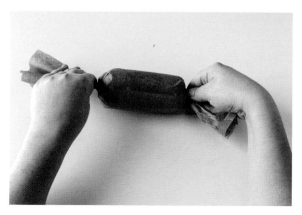

Roll the log up in the parchment and twist the ends of the parchment in opposite directions, as if it's a piece of candy. Refrigerate until firm.

SHAPING COMPOUND BUTTERS

You have several options:

- Transfer the flavored butter to a sheet of parchment paper, roll tightly into a 1½-inch-thick log (a straight edge is helpful for forming an even log), and twist both ends of the parchment paper to seal. Slip the log into a paper towel tube if company's coming and you want it to be perfectly round, and refrigerate until firm. To serve, cut slices of flavored butter with a warm knife (simply run hot water over the blade and then wipe it dry).

- Serve the butter by the scoop or by the dollop directly from the mixing bowl.

- Pack the butter into small ramekins or individual butter crocks, cover with plastic wrap, and refrigerate. Bring the butter to room temperature before serving.

- Fill a pastry bag fitted with a star tip with the flavored butter and pipe rosettes onto a parchment-lined baking tray. Refrigerate until firm, then cover with plastic wrap. When they're firm, the rosettes will pop right off the parchment. You can also pipe rosettes directly onto a finished dish.

- Butter molds or silicone ice cube trays, which come in a variety of shapes, are another fun option.

- If you really want to get creative, spread the compound butter in a ½-inch-thick layer on a parchment-lined baking tray, refrigerate until firm, and cut out shapes using small cookie cutters.

- Finally, a log of cold compound butter that has been out of the refrigerator for about 15 minutes can be shaped using a warm butter curler or melon baller. Keep butter curls or balls chilled in ice water until it's time to serve them.

  Note: Chunky compound butters are not suitable for piping, molding, cookie-cutter shapes, or curling.

Clarified Butter

Clarified butter—sometimes called drawn butter—is butter minus the water and milk solids. In other words, it's pure butterfat.

Plain clarified butter is used for high-heat cooking such as searing and sautéing since removing the milk solids raises the smoke point. Flavored clarified butter can be used either as a cooking fat or for finishing dishes. Possibly the best-known flavored clarified butter is Garlic Drawn Butter (page 69), which is served as an accompaniment to seafood.

TOOLS AND EQUIPMENT FOR CLARIFIED BUTTER

- *Small, heavy saucepan.* This is best for melting the butter.
- *Fine-mesh skimmer or shallow-bowled spoon.* Use this for skimming off the foam that rises to the surface of the melted butter.
- *Small ladle.* You'll need this for ladling the pure butterfat off the milky liquid below.
- *Fine-mesh sieve and cheesecloth.* Use these for straining.

Making Clarified Butter

It's easiest to clarify butter when you start with at least 1 pound of butter and use a tall, narrow saucepan.

To make clarified butter, gently melt unsalted butter in a small, heavy saucepan over low heat, using a fine-mesh skimmer or a shallow-bowled spoon to skim off any foam that rises to the surface. Do not stir or otherwise agitate the melting butter. Remove the pan from the heat and let rest for about 15 minutes to allow the milk solids to settle to the bottom of the pan. You will see two distinct layers form—a layer of clear butterfat floating atop a layer of milky liquid. Carefully ladle the butterfat off the milky liquid and you have clarified butter. One pound of butter will yield 11 to 12 ounces (about 1½ cups) of clarified butter, depending on how much patience you have. The milky liquid that remains can be discarded or used in baked goods.

An alternative method results in clarified butter with a hint of toastiness. Melt unsalted butter in a small, heavy saucepan over low heat until it boils. Simmer until all of the water content has cooked away and the milk solids barely begin to brown, skimming off any foam that rises to the surface. Strain through a cheesecloth-lined fine-mesh sieve to remove the milk solids. This type of clarified butter is a common ingredient in Indian cooking and is referred to as *ghee*.

Clarified butter can be infused with any number of flavorings, including herbs, spices, garlic, and even crustacean shells. Sometimes the clarified butter is heated with the flavoring for a more intense infusion. The process is basically the same as infusing oil.

Butter separates into foam, butterfat, and milky liquid when melted.

Storing Clarified Butter

Pure clarified butter can be kept at room temperature, but since just the slightest speck of milk solids can cause spoilage, I prefer storing it in the refrigerator. Tightly sealed plain clarified butter will keep for months in the refrigerator or almost indefinitely in the freezer. Clarified butter that has been flavored with raw fresh ingredients such as garlic has the same keeping properties as compound butter—several days tightly sealed in the refrigerator or several weeks in the freezer. Clarified butter that has been infused with flavor through cooking keeps for several weeks tightly sealed in the refrigerator or several months in the freezer.

Brown Butter

Brown butter is butter that has been cooked until the water content cooks away and the milk solids brown. It has a lovely nutty flavor and is therefore sometimes called *beurre noisette*, literally "hazelnut butter" in French.

Brown butter is used with or without additional flavorings as a sauce for fish, gnocchi, ravioli, and vegetables. It is also used in many baked goods such as financiers.

TOOLS AND EQUIPMENT FOR BROWN BUTTER
- *Small, heavy saucepan.* Again, this is best for heating butter.
- *Wooden spoon.* A metal spoon will get too hot to handle.

Making Brown Butter

To make brown butter, cook unsalted butter in a small, heavy saucepan over moderate heat, stirring constantly. The butter will melt, then foam as the water cooks away, and then begin to color. Remove the pan from the heat when the butter is a deep brown and has a toasty, nutty aroma. The residual heat of the pan can cause the butter to go from brown to black in a matter of moments, so immediately stop the cooking by adding other ingredients, such as herbs, spices, shallots, and acid, dipping the bottom of the pan into an ice bath for a second or two, or pouring the brown butter out of the pan.

Storing Brown Butter

Plain and flavored brown butter will keep for several days tightly sealed in the refrigerator or several weeks in the freezer.

Savory
BUTTERS

I've organized these recipes according to the
cuisines that inspired them. American and
European flavors come first. Then come ideas
from Mexico and from Asia. Clarified and brown-
butter recipes conclude the chapter.

ESSENTIAL GARLIC BUTTER
MAKES 8 SERVINGS

*T*here's nothing better than this slathered on a fresh baguette. But this butter is also truly the trick up my sleeve on nights when I'm too busy or too tired to worry about dinner. As a convenience "sauce," it'll make anything and everything—beef, pork, lamb, chicken, seafood, starch, or vegetable that's been seared, sautéed, baked, roasted, broiled, or grilled—taste fantastic. It can be spread on fish or under the skin of chicken before cooking, and it's ideal for making garlic bread. It can be used to embellish plain foods as well as dishes that have been marinated or rubbed with spices. With the addition of herbs, it can even be used to make such dishes as Chicken Kiev, baked oysters, and escargots. It is the butter to have in the refrigerator at all times.

> 8 tablespoons (1 stick) unsalted butter, softened
> 2 large garlic cloves, grated on a Microplane
> ¼ teaspoon *fleur de sel* or other finishing sea salt, or to taste

Blend together the butter, garlic, and salt in a medium-size bowl. Form into a log and refrigerate until firm before slicing and serving, or use another shaping method (see pages 16–17).

VARIATION
• *Garlic-Herb Butter:* Blend in 2 tablespoons minced fresh herbs such as flat-leaf parsley, thyme, basil, oregano, rosemary, and/or sage.

SHALLOT-HERB BUTTER
MAKES 8 SERVINGS

This all-purpose butter is similar to Essential Garlic Butter (opposite), but it's less pungent. Use it whenever a subtler flavor is desired. You can vary the herbs as you like.

8 tablespoons (1 stick) unsalted butter, softened
1 small shallot, minced (see page 92)
1 tablespoon minced flat-leaf parsley
1 teaspoon minced fresh thyme
1 teaspoon minced fresh rosemary
¼ teaspoon kosher salt, or to taste
Generous pinch of freshly ground black pepper

Blend together the butter, shallot, parsley, thyme, rosemary, salt, and pepper in a medium-size bowl. Form into a log and refrigerate until firm before slicing and serving, or use another shaping method (see pages 16–17).

"Dropping a lozenge of compound herb butter onto a steak or baked potato elevates humble victuals into seriously good eats."

—Alton Brown, *Good Eats: The Early Years* (2009)

MAÎTRE D'HÔTEL BUTTER

A t one time or another, a version of this compound but-ter has appeared on nearly every fine-dining restaurant menu. It's exceedingly simple, but thanks to that little bit of lemon juice, it really enlivens steamed vegetables and fish preparations.

> 8 tablespoons (1 stick) unsalted butter, softened
> 2 tablespoons minced flat-leaf parsley
> 2 tablespoons freshly squeezed lemon juice
> ¼ teaspoon kosher salt, or to taste

Blend together the butter, parsley, lemon juice, and salt in a medium-size bowl. Form into a log and refrigerate until firm before slicing and serving, or use another shaping method (see pages 16–17).

DILL, LEMON, AND GARLIC BUTTER
MAKES 8 SERVINGS

*D*ill and seafood is a classic flavor pairing, so this butter is perfect for fish fillets, shrimp, and scallops. You can add it either before or after cooking.

8 tablespoons (1 stick) unsalted butter, softened
¼ cup minced fresh dill
1 garlic clove, grated on a Microplane
1 teaspoon grated lemon zest
2 tablespoons freshly squeezed lemon juice
¼ teaspoon kosher salt, or to taste
Generous pinch of freshly ground black pepper

Blend together the butter, dill, garlic, zest, lemon juice, salt, and pepper in a medium-size bowl. Form into a log and refrigerate until firm before slicing and serving, or use another shaping method (see pages 16–17).

"This magical, mystical gift from the cow makes almost *everything* taste better."
—Michael Ruhlman, *Ruhlman's Twenty* (2011)

ROSEMARY–ROASTED GARLIC BUTTER
MAKES 8 SERVINGS

An entire head of sweet and mellow roasted garlic can be used to flavor a single stick of butter. There's no need to mince the garlic before incorporating it into the butter because it will be soft enough to blend in smoothly.

Pork chops and lamb chops are delightful topped with this butter—as are mashed potatoes.

1 head garlic
1 tablespoon extra-virgin olive oil
8 tablespoons (1 stick) unsalted butter, softened
1 teaspoon minced fresh rosemary
¼ teaspoon kosher salt, or to taste

Preheat the oven to 350°F. Cut the stem end off the head of garlic to expose the cloves within. Place the garlic in the center of a piece of aluminum foil, drizzle with the oil, and seal the foil tightly. Roast for 40 to 45 minutes, or until the garlic is meltingly tender and golden brown. Let cool to room temperature. Peel off all the papery skins.

Blend together the roasted garlic, butter, rosemary, and salt in a medium-size bowl. Form into a log and refrigerate until firm before slicing and serving, or use another shaping method (see pages 16–17).

MINT BUTTER

The sprightly freshness of this butter can go with a variety of dishes. Lamb and pea preparations are a particularly good match. But if you omit the garlic, it can be served with sweet items such as berry scones or baguette-and-melted-chocolate sandwiches.

> 8 tablespoons (1 stick) unsalted butter, softened
> 2 tablespoons minced fresh mint
> 1 tablespoon freshly squeezed lemon juice
> 1 garlic clove (optional), grated on a Microplane
> ¼ teaspoon kosher salt, or to taste

Blend together the butter, mint, lemon juice, garlic (if using), and salt in a medium-size bowl. Form into a log and refrigerate until firm before slicing and serving, or use another shaping method (see pages 16–17).

> "I think of flavored butters as a modern convenience form of hollandaise or béarnaise sauce, just cutting a frozen slice to use on grilled food instead of whipping up yolks and butter."
>
> —Jacques Pépin, Julia and Jacques Cooking at Home (1999)

TARRAGON BUTTER
MAKES 8 SERVINGS

*F*resh tarragon has an assertive anise-like flavor. Try the chervil variation if you prefer something subtler.

Use this butter as an easy alternative to béarnaise sauce with grilled steak. Or serve it with lobster; tarragon and lobster is a classic flavor pairing.

> 8 tablespoons (1 stick) unsalted butter, softened
> 1 tablespoon minced fresh tarragon
> ¼ teaspoon kosher salt, or to taste

Blend together the butter, tarragon, and salt in a medium-size bowl. Form into a log and refrigerate until firm before slicing and serving, or use another shaping method (see pages 16–17).

VARIATION
• *Chervil Butter:* Substitute 2 tablespoons minced fresh chervil for the tarragon.

CARAMELIZED ONION BUTTER

MAKES 8 SERVINGS

S low and low is the key to caramelizing onions. Gentle cooking transforms onions from positively pungent to golden brown, sweet, and mellow. They make a delicious stand-alone topping for burgers or steak, but blending them into butter makes them even better.

Serve this butter atop steak, stuff it into burger patties, toss it with steamed or roasted vegetables, or stir it into mashed potatoes and grain dishes.

2 tablespoons extra-virgin olive oil
1 yellow onion, julienned (see page 92)
8 tablespoons (1 stick) unsalted butter, softened
¼ teaspoon kosher salt, or to taste

Heat a medium-size, heavy sauté pan over medium-low heat. Add the oil and the onion and cook, stirring frequently, for 50 to 55 minutes, or until the onion is caramelized. Let cool to room temperature. Combine the caramelized onions, butter, and salt in a food processor and pulse until smooth. Form into a log and refrigerate until firm before slicing and serving, or use another shaping method (see pages 16–17).

HORSERADISH BUTTER
MAKES 8 SERVINGS

*B*utter brings out the flavor of horseradish while taming its sinus-burning qualities. Beef and horseradish is a classic combination, so naturally this butter is good on roast beef sandwiches, steaks, and even prime rib.

8 tablespoons (1 stick) unsalted butter, softened
2 tablespoons prepared horseradish, drained
½ teaspoon Worcestershire sauce
¼ teaspoon kosher salt, or to taste

Blend together the butter, horseradish, Worcestershire, and salt in a medium-size bowl. Form into a log and refrigerate until firm before slicing and serving, or use another shaping method (see pages 16–17).

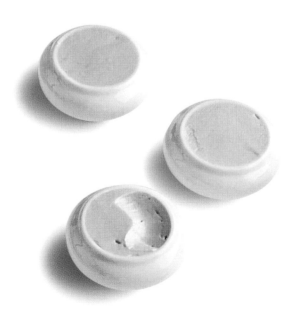

FENNEL BUTTER

MAKES 8 SERVINGS

*T*his butter has a special affinity with pork—use it to sauce any fresh pork preparation such as seared, grilled, or roasted chops or tenderloins or sautéed cutlets. It also works well with chicken, veal, lamb, and seafood.

8 tablespoons (1 stick) unsalted butter, softened
1 garlic clove, grated on a Microplane
1 teaspoon freshly squeezed lemon juice
1 teaspoon fennel seeds, toasted and ground (see page 11)
¼ teaspoon kosher salt, or to taste
Generous pinch of hot red pepper flakes

Blend together the butter, garlic, lemon juice, fennel seeds, salt, and hot pepper flakes in a medium-size bowl. Form into a log and refrigerate until firm before slicing and serving, or use another shaping method (see pages 16–17).

GORGONZOLA-CHIVE BUTTER

MAKES 8 SERVINGS

I use Gorgonzola dolce—which is a mild, sweet variety of blue cheese—in this recipe, because it's creamy and blends almost, but not completely, into the butter. However, any type of blue cheese will do.

Top a grilled or seared steak with a generous pat of this butter for a meal worthy of the best steak house. Blue cheese lovers will also enjoy this butter stuffed inside hamburger patties or as a sauce for gnocchi.

8 tablespoons (1 stick) unsalted butter, softened
4 ounces Gorgonzola dolce, crumbled (about ⅔ cup lightly packed)
2 tablespoons minced fresh chives
⅛ teaspoon kosher salt, or to taste

Blend together the butter, Gorgonzola, chives, and salt in a medium-size bowl. Form into a log and refrigerate until firm before slicing and serving, or use another shaping method (see pages 16–17).

SMOKED BUTTER
MAKES 8 SERVINGS

*T*his butter isn't truly smoked—it just tastes like it is. It gets its subtle smokiness from finely ground smoked sea salt, which is available at many gourmet markets. Use it to embellish the flavor of grilled or cedar-planked foods such as salmon, chicken, or vegetables.

½ teaspoon smoked sea salt
8 tablespoons (1 stick) unsalted butter, softened
Generous pinch of freshly ground black pepper
Generous pinch of cayenne pepper

Grind the salt to a fine powder with a mortar and pestle or a spice mill. Blend together the salt, butter, black pepper, and cayenne in a medium-size bowl. Form into a log and refrigerate until firm before slicing and serving, or use another shaping method (see pages 16–17).

> "Here is a truism that makes the uncertainties and stresses of life a little more manageable: few things cannot be made better with the addition of a little (more) butter. All cooks should rejoice in this happy circumstance."
> —Michael Ruhlman, *Ruhlman's Twenty* (2011)

PORCINI BUTTER
MAKES 8 SERVINGS

*T*he concentrated earthy flavor of dried porcini mushrooms makes them ideal for use in a flavored butter.
When purchasing dried porcini, avoid those with pinholes,
which are a sure sign of worms. Good-quality ones are available in most gourmet markets.

Serve this butter on grilled steak, tuck it into baked potatoes or whip it into mashed ones, toss it with fresh egg pasta,
stir it into risotto, or add it to any button mushroom dish for
a flavor boost.

¼ ounce dried porcini mushrooms
8 tablespoons (1 stick) unsalted butter, softened
¼ teaspoon minced fresh thyme
¼ teaspoon *fleur de sel* or other finishing sea salt, or to taste
Generous pinch of freshly ground black pepper

Grind the dried porcini to a fine powder in a blender or spice
mill. Blend together the porcini powder, butter, thyme, salt,
and pepper in a medium-size bowl. Form into a log and refrigerate until firm before slicing and serving, or use another
shaping method (see pages 16–17).

VARIATION
• *Shiitake Butter:* Substitute dried shiitake mushrooms for the porcini and
omit the thyme.

PORT BUTTER

MAKES 8 SERVINGS

*T*his butter appeared in my first cookbook, *Seared to Perfection*, but since it's one of my favorites I had to include it here, too. I like to serve it on romantic occasions. On Valentine's Day, I have used a small heart-shaped cookie cutter to cut out pink "melting hearts" to top seared tenderloin steaks. The balsamic variation complements lamb chops well.

½ cup ruby port
1 shallot, minced (see page 92)
1 sprig fresh thyme
4 black peppercorns
8 tablespoons (1 stick) unsalted butter, softened
¼ teaspoon kosher salt, or to taste

Combine the port, shallot, thyme, and peppercorns in a small saucepan. Bring to a boil, then reduce the heat and simmer until very thick and syrupy, 7 or 8 minutes. Strain through a fine-mesh sieve and let cool to room temperature.

Blend together the port reduction, butter, and salt in a medium-size bowl. Form into a log and refrigerate until firm before slicing and serving, or use another shaping method (see pages 16–17).

VARIATION

• *Balsamic Butter:* Substitute balsamic vinegar for the port.

OLIVE BUTTER

MAKES 8 SERVINGS

Even as a little girl I understood that butter and olives belonged together. One of my favorite snacks was black olives stuffed with unsalted butter (I kid you not—my grandparents fed it to me!). While I don't necessarily suggest it as an hors d'oeuvre for your next dinner party, I do recommend the combination in the form of a compound butter. The saltiness of the olives and the sweetness of the butter come together in perfect harmony. A mix of black and green Cerignola olives is my favorite for this recipe, but you can experiment with your own variations.

It's delicious melting over sautéed chicken, turkey, pork, veal cutlets, or fish fillets.

8 tablespoons (1 stick) unsalted butter, softened
1½ ounces pitted black olives (about ⅓ cup)
1½ ounces pitted green olives (about ⅓ cup)

Combine the butter and olives in a food processor and pulse until smooth. Form into a log and refrigerate until firm before slicing and serving, or use another shaping method (see pages 16–17).

ANCHOVY BUTTER
MAKES 8 SERVINGS

Seafood is an obvious use for this butter, but you'd be surprised by how well it goes with grilled steaks. That's because anchovies are an umami-rich ingredient, and just a small quantity will amp up meaty flavors.

8 tablespoons (1 stick) unsalted butter, softened
4 anchovy fillets, minced
2 tablespoons minced flat-leaf parsley
1 garlic clove, grated on a Microplane
1 teaspoon freshly squeezed lemon juice
¼ teaspoon kosher salt, or to taste
Generous pinch of freshly ground black pepper

Blend together the butter, anchovies, parsley, garlic, lemon juice, salt, and pepper in a medium-size bowl. Form into a log and refrigerate until firm before slicing and serving, or use another shaping method (see pages 16–17).

CAVIAR BUTTER

MAKES 8 SERVINGS

*T*he typical Russian open-faced sandwich of salmon roe and unsalted butter on a slice of bread—a part of every proper *zakuski* (appetizer) spread—is the inspiration for this butter. You can make it with either black caviar or salmon roe, which is of course a more affordable luxury. I recommend spreading it on a toasted bagel or a slice of French bread. It can also give soft-boiled eggs and baked potatoes a touch of elegance. Russian markets are a good source for both red and black caviar.

Make sure that the butter is *very* soft when you make this recipe, and blend the ingredients gently so that you don't pop the caviar.

8 tablespoons (1 stick) unsalted butter, softened
½ to 1 ounce caviar

Gently blend together the butter and caviar in a medium-size bowl. Form into a log and refrigerate until firm before slicing and serving, or use another shaping method (see pages 16–17). This butter should be very soft when served as a spread.

TRUFFLED FOIE GRAS BUTTER

MAKES 8 SERVINGS

*T*here's just enough truffle here to come through without overwhelming the delicate foie gras, but if you'd like a more assertive truffle flavor, substitute additional truffle salt for the *fleur de sel*. Using a fine-mesh sieve rather than a food processor to puree the foie gras removes any veins or gristly bits. This sort of butter can also be made using the fat that renders from seared foie gras.

I have a local butcher who sells foie gras by the slice, so check with your butcher. But you can also purchase foie gras online. Slice and sear any of the liver you don't use for the butter; I've got a recipe in my book *Seared to Perfection* (The Harvard Common Press, 2010).

This is a luxurious, special-occasion butter to be served with brioche toast points, caviar, and champagne. It's also an indulgent topping for steaks.

4 ounces fresh foie gras
¼ teaspoon truffle salt
Generous pinch of freshly ground white pepper
8 tablespoons (1 stick) unsalted butter, softened
¼ teaspoon *fleur de sel* or other finishing sea salt, or to taste

The day before you plan to make the butter, season the foie gras with the truffle salt and white pepper. Cover with plastic wrap and refrigerate overnight. Remove the foie gras from the refrigerator and set aside at room temperature for 45 minutes to 1 hour, or until just soft. Meanwhile, heat a large pot of water over medium heat to a bare simmer. Transfer the foie gras to a sheet of plastic wrap, roll tightly into a 1¾-inch-thick log, and tie both ends of the plastic wrap with butcher's twine.

Place the wrapped foie gras log in the barely simmering water and poach for 1 to 2 minutes, or until soft and beginning to melt. Transfer to an ice bath and chill for 10 to 15 minutes, or until just firm. Remove from the ice bath and wipe dry. Unwrap the foie gras and force it through a fine-mesh sieve.

Blend together the foie gras puree, butter, and *fleur de sel* in a medium-size bowl. Form into a log and refrigerate until firm before slicing and serving, or use another shaping method (see pages 16–17).

> "Good bread is the most fundamentally satisfying of all foods; and good bread with fresh butter, the greatest of feasts."
> —James Beard

RADISH BUTTER
MAKES 8 SERVINGS

*T*he favorite French snack of radishes with butter and *fleur de sel* inspired this recipe. It's a simple combination, yet the play of peppery and sweet with the zing of crunchy salt is irresistible when spread on a fresh baguette.

> 8 tablespoons (1 stick) unsalted butter, preferably cultured, softened
> 2 ounces radishes, preferably French breakfast radishes, finely diced
> ¼ teaspoon *fleur de sel* or other finishing sea salt, or to taste

Blend together the butter, radishes, and salt in a medium-size bowl. Form into a log and refrigerate until firm before slicing and serving, or use another shaping method (see pages 16–17). Don't freeze this butter.

VARIATION
- *Radish-Herb Butter:* Blend in 2 tablespoons minced fresh tender herbs such as chives, flat-leaf parsley, chervil, dill, basil, and/or mint.

GOAT CHEESE AND SUN-DRIED TOMATO BUTTER

MAKES 8 SERVINGS

A trip to sunny Provence inspired this butter. It makes a vibrant sauce for chicken, fish, and pasta dishes, and it can also be used as a spread for steak sandwiches. Consider trying goat's milk butter instead of cow's milk butter in this recipe.

8 sun-dried tomato halves
8 tablespoons (1 stick) unsalted butter or goat's milk butter, softened
3 ounces fresh chèvre
1 garlic clove, grated on a Microplane
½ teaspoon *herbes de Provence* (see Source Guide, page 92)
¼ teaspoon kosher salt, or to taste
Generous pinch of freshly ground black pepper

Place the sun-dried tomatoes in a bowl, add enough boiling water to cover, and let soak for 10 to 12 minutes, or until rehydrated. Transfer the tomatoes to a paper towel–lined plate and drain for about a minute.

Combine the tomatoes, butter, chèvre, garlic, *herbes de Provence*, salt, and pepper in a food processor and pulse until smooth. Form into a log and refrigerate until firm before slicing and serving, or use another shaping method (see pages 16–17).

VARIATIONS

- *Goat Cheese, Sun-Dried Tomato, and Caper Butter:* Blend in 1 tablespoon drained capers. This variation is not suitable for piping, molding, cookie-cutter shapes, or curling.
- *Goat Cheese, Sun-Dried Tomato, and Olive Butter:* Blend in ½ ounce (about 2 tablespoons) chopped pitted green olives. This variation is not suitable for piping, molding, cookie-cutter shapes, or curling.

TARTINE BUTTER

MAKES 8 SERVINGS

A *tartine* is a French sandwich. From what I can tell, *tartines* are the most popular fast food in Paris; every café has a selection of prepared *tartines* piled high in a display case, and people grab them to go, eating as they dash about the city. These sandwiches are made with a variety of fillings, but one thing they all have in common is a generous smear of butter. My favorite *tartine* is the ham and Swiss cheese with butter and mustard on fresh baguette. It may seem mundane but trust me: When prepared with ingredients of the highest quality, it is indeed a delicacy. Make your own *tartines* using this flavored butter. I did not include any salt in the recipe because I like how sweet butter contrasts with salty cold cuts, but feel free to add *fleur de sel* if you wish.

8 tablespoons (1 stick) unsalted butter, preferably cultured, softened
1 tablespoon plus 1 teaspoon Dijon mustard

Blend together the butter and mustard in a medium-size bowl. Form into a log and refrigerate until firm before slicing and serving, or use another shaping method (see pages 16–17).

PARMIGIANO BUTTER

MAKES 8 SERVINGS

What's not to love about the combination of sweet butter and the "king of cheeses"? I'll eat it on pasta, I'll eat it on green veggies—heck, I'll eat it on its own! But seriously, orzo mixed with a pat of this butter has been a quick and comforting dinner at my house on a number of occasions, and it's a favorite topping for blanched asparagus in the springtime. It can also be used to make killer pita chips—just spread lightly on split pita bread and toast until crisp and golden brown.

Real Parmigiano-Reggiano is a necessity here, and it must be finely grated, preferably with a Microplane, so that it melts into the butter.

> 8 tablespoons (1 stick) unsalted butter, softened
> 1 ounce (about ⅔ cup lightly packed) freshly grated Parmigiano-Reggiano
> 1 garlic clove, grated on a Microplane
> ⅛ teaspoon kosher salt, or to taste
> Generous pinch of freshly ground black pepper
> Generous pinch of freshly ground nutmeg

Blend together the butter, cheese, garlic, salt, pepper, and nutmeg in a medium-size bowl. Form into a log and refrigerate until firm before slicing and serving, or use another shaping method (see pages 16–17).

BASIL PESTO BUTTER
MAKES 8 SERVINGS

It's very unorthodox to make pesto with butter instead of olive oil, but why not break the rules sometimes?

The applications for pesto butter are endless. Use it to spread on panini, to garnish minestrone, and to top grilled steak or roasted chicken or lamb. For a quick weeknight meal, slather it generously on fish fillets, scatter cherry tomatoes all around, roast in a hot oven, and serve over a bed of pasta. If you need a shortcut, simply stir a few tablespoons of store-bought pesto into softened butter.

8 tablespoons (1 stick) unsalted butter, softened
1½ cups lightly packed fresh basil leaves
½ ounce (about ⅓ cup lightly packed) freshly grated Parmigiano-Reggiano
2 tablespoons pine nuts
1 garlic clove, grated on a Microplane
⅛ teaspoon kosher salt, or to taste

Combine the butter, basil, cheese, pine nuts, garlic, and salt in a food processor and pulse until smooth. Form into a log and refrigerate until firm before slicing and serving, or use another shaping method (see pages 16–17).

VARIATION
• *Arugula Pesto Butter:* Substitute baby arugula for the basil.

SAFFRON-PIMENTÓN BUTTER
MAKES 8 SERVINGS

*T*he flavors of Spain inspire this smoky, red-hued butter. Smoky *pimentón*, or Spanish paprika, is available in both sweet and hot varieties. I opt for the sweet version, so the heat doesn't overwhelm the flavor when it's used in quantity.

Sauté shrimp or mussels in this butter, spread it under the skin of a chicken to be roasted, or use it to flavor the rice in *arroz con pollo*.

> 8 tablespoons (1 stick) unsalted butter, softened
> 1 garlic clove, grated on a Microplane
> 1 teaspoon sweet *pimentón* (Spanish paprika; see Source Guide, page 92)
> ¼ teaspoon kosher salt
> Generous pinch of saffron

Blend together the butter, garlic, *pimentón*, salt, and saffron in a medium-size bowl. Form into a log and refrigerate until firm before slicing and serving, or use another shaping method (see pages 16–17).

CHIPOTLE BUTTER

MAKES 8 SERVINGS

If you like your food to have a little heat, this is sure to become one of your favorite butters. It's spicy and smoky, and when you pair it with grilled food, it can't be beat. Marbled rib-eye steaks and corn on the cob are both good candidates for a pat. The lime variation is a good match for grilled salmon and shrimp. Use more or fewer chipotles as you wish to adjust the heat level. Leftover chipotles keep well frozen.

4 chipotles in adobo sauce
8 tablespoons (1 stick) unsalted butter, softened
1 garlic clove, grated on a Microplane
¼ teaspoon kosher salt, or to taste
Generous pinch of ground cumin

Force the chipotles through a fine-mesh sieve to remove the skins and seeds. Blend together the chipotle puree, butter, garlic, salt, and cumin in a medium-size bowl. Form into a log and refrigerate until firm before slicing and serving, or use another shaping method (see pages 16–17).

VARIATION

- *Chipotle-Lime Butter:* Blend in 2 teaspoons freshly squeezed lime juice and 1 teaspoon grated lime zest.

RED CHILE BUTTER

MAKES 8 SERVINGS

All three dried chiles used in this recipe are mild in terms of heat, but each one brings a distinct flavor to the mix. They can be found at Mexican markets and some gourmet grocery stores.

Steak, pork chops, salmon, shrimp, roasted winter squash, baked sweet potatoes, corn on the cob, warm corn or flour tortillas, and popcorn are all good uses for this earthy, Mexican-inspired butter.

1 ancho chile, stemmed
1 pasilla chile, stemmed
1 guajillo chile, stemmed
8 tablespoons (1 stick) unsalted butter, softened
1 garlic clove, grated on a Microplane
¼ teaspoon kosher salt, or to taste
⅛ teaspoon ground cumin

Heat a medium-size, heavy sauté pan or griddle over medium heat until very hot. Add the chiles and toast, pressing down on them firmly with a spatula, for 10 to 15 seconds, or until golden brown. Turn the chiles and continue to toast, pressing down on them firmly with the spatula, another 10 to 15 seconds, or until fragrant, golden brown, and pliable. Remove the toasted chiles to a bowl, add enough boiling water to cover, and let soak for 10 to 12 minutes, or until rehydrated. Transfer the chiles and 2 tablespoons of the soaking liquid to a blender and blend until smooth. Force the chiles through a fine-mesh sieve to remove the skins and seeds.

Blend together the chile puree, butter, garlic, salt, and cumin in a medium-size bowl. Form into a log and refrigerate until firm before slicing and serving, or use another shaping method (see pages 16–17).

MISO-SCALLION BUTTER
MAKES 8 SERVINGS

miso, a mainstay of Japanese cuisine, is fermented soybean paste that's both salty and umami. Butter flavored with miso can best be described as savory, brothy, mouth-filling, rich, meaty, hearty, and satisfying. Spread it on fish fillets and bake or broil them. Or try it on grilled or seared steak, pork, chicken, or seafood served over sticky rice and vegetables, rice bowl–style.

Asian markets and most well-stocked grocery stores carry miso.

8 tablespoons (1 stick) unsalted butter, softened
2 tablespoons miso, preferably red
2 tablespoons finely sliced scallions

Blend together the butter, miso, and scallions in a medium-size bowl. Form into a log and refrigerate until firm before slicing and serving, or use another shaping method (see pages 16–17).

VARIATION
• *Sesame-Miso-Scallion Butter:* Blend in 2 teaspoons toasted sesame seeds and ½ teaspoon toasted sesame oil.

WASABI BUTTER
MAKES 8 SERVINGS

*T*his butter has all the flavor and little of the pungency of wasabi. For a little East-meets-West fusion, try a pat melting atop seared ahi tuna or grilled rib-eye or New York strip steaks.

When purchasing wasabi powder, look for a brand that actually includes wasabi in the ingredient list—most brands are horseradish with coloring and contain no wasabi at all.

8 tablespoons (1 stick) unsalted butter, softened
2 tablespoons wasabi powder
2 teaspoons soy sauce

Blend together the butter, wasabi, and soy sauce in a medium-size bowl. Form into a log and refrigerate until firm before slicing and serving, or use another shaping method (see pages 16–17).

"As for butter versus margarine, I trust cows more than chemists."

—Joan Gussow

GREEN TEA–SESAME BUTTER

MAKES 8 SERVINGS

*T*his green-hued butter is flavored primarily with matcha tea, which gives it a subtly sweet vegetal note that complements both sweet and savory foods. It pairs nicely with seafood—particularly salmon fillets—and steamed vegetables. But it's also delicious spread on ginger scones.

Matcha is the powdered green tea traditionally used in the Japanese tea ceremony and can be found at tea shops, many Asian markets, and online (see Source Guide, page 92).

> 8 tablespoons (1 stick) unsalted butter, softened
> 2 teaspoons matcha tea, sifted
> 2 teaspoons toasted sesame seeds (use black sesame seeds if you want to see the speckles)
> 2 teaspoons sugar
> ¼ teaspoon kosher salt, or to taste
> ⅛ teaspoon toasted sesame oil

Blend together the butter, tea, sesame seeds, sugar, salt, and sesame oil in a medium-size bowl. Form into a log and refrigerate until firm before slicing and serving, or use another shaping method (see pages 16–17).

KIMCHI BUTTER
MAKES 8 SERVINGS

*T*he national pickle of Korea, kimchi is fermented napa cabbage with plenty of red chile. It's pungent and spicy, making this butter a great topping for grilled beef.

Kimchi is available at Asian markets and most grocery stores.

8 tablespoons (1 stick) unsalted butter, softened
2 ounces (about ¼ cup) kimchi
2 tablespoons sliced scallions (white and green parts)
1 teaspoon soy sauce

Combine the butter, kimchi, scallions, and soy sauce in a food processor and pulse until smooth. Form into a log and refrigerate until firm before slicing and serving, or use another shaping method (see pages 16–17).

GINGER BUTTER
MAKES 8 SERVINGS

*G*inger gives this butter a lovely freshness. Consider it as a topping for such vegetables as carrots, snow peas, or bok choy; on such seafood as shrimp, scallops, or crab; or on fish fillets, whether bold like salmon or mild like tilapia.

8 tablespoons (1 stick) unsalted butter, softened
2 teaspoons grated fresh ginger
1 teaspoon soy sauce
1 teaspoon honey, preferably orange blossom

Blend together the butter, ginger, soy sauce, and honey in a medium-size bowl. Form into a log and refrigerate until firm before slicing and serving, or use another shaping method (see pages 16–17).

CORIANDER-TOMATO BUTTER

MAKES 8 SERVINGS

*T*he spices in this butter are vaguely reminiscent of Middle Eastern or Indian cooking, so try it with lamb, chicken, shrimp, or fish with basmati rice or garbanzo beans. Toasting and grinding the spices fresh brings out their aroma and flavor. However, preground spices may be used if whole ones are not available.

8 tablespoons (1 stick) unsalted butter, softened
2 teaspoons coriander seeds, toasted and ground (see page 11)
¼ teaspoon cumin seeds, toasted and ground (see page 11)
2 tablespoons tomato paste
2 tablespoons minced fresh cilantro
1 garlic clove, grated on a Microplane
¼ teaspoon kosher salt, or to taste

Blend together the butter, coriander, cumin, tomato paste, cilantro, garlic, and salt in a medium-size bowl. Form into a log and refrigerate until firm before slicing and serving, or use another shaping method (see pages 16–17).

CURRY BUTTER

MAKES 8 SERVINGS

Use this bold butter when you'd like to add a bit of Indian flavor to your meal. It pairs well with lamb, fish, cauliflower, spinach, lentils, and basmati rice.

8 tablespoons (1 stick) unsalted butter, softened
2 tablespoons minced fresh cilantro
2 teaspoons curry powder
2 teaspoons freshly squeezed lime juice
1 teaspoon grated fresh ginger
1 garlic clove, grated on a Microplane
¼ teaspoon kosher salt, or to taste

Blend together the butter, cilantro, curry powder, lime juice, ginger, garlic, and salt in a medium-size bowl. Form into a log and refrigerate until firm before slicing and serving, or use another shaping method (see pages 16–17).

GARLIC DRAWN BUTTER

MAKES 8 SERVINGS

This butter is the essential accompaniment for steamed seafood dinners. You can't have crab legs or lobster tails without it. The lemon variation makes a good dip for steamed artichokes.

> 6 ounces (¾ cup) clarified butter (see page 18), melted
> 2 garlic cloves, grated on a Microplane

Combine the butter and garlic in a jar. Cover and refrigerate overnight. To serve, transfer to a small, heavy saucepan and heat until melted. Strain through a fine-mesh sieve. Serve the warm butter in a butter warmer, small fondue pot, or individual dipping cups.

This butter will keep for several days tightly sealed in the refrigerator or several weeks in the freezer.

VARIATION

• *Garlic-Lemon Drawn Butter:* Add 1½ teaspoons grated lemon zest along with the garlic.

SHRIMP BUTTER
MAKES 10 OUNCES, APPROXIMATELY 12 TO 14 SERVINGS

Whenever you prepare shrimp, save the shells in the freezer in a zipper-top plastic bag, and when you've accumulated enough, make a batch of this butter. You can also use crawfish, crab, or lobster shells. Chopping the shells fine in a food processor minimizes their volume, allowing for the maximum amount to be used to flavor the butter. It would be impractical to make a small quantity so the recipe makes a lot, but fortunately it keeps well.

Since this boldly flavored, coral-colored condiment is made from clarified butter, it can be used for both cooking and finishing. It's extremely versatile. Sauté seafood in it; make a roux for seafood soups and stews with it; toss a spoonful into a seafood pasta; stir some into seafood risotto; or—and this is my favorite application—drizzle it over seafood bisque right before serving. A little bit will go a long way toward pumping up the seafood flavor.

> 4 ounces shrimp shells
> 12 ounces (1½ cups) clarified butter (page 18), melted
> 1 garlic clove
> 5 black peppercorns
> 1 allspice berry
> 1 bay leaf

Pulse the shrimp shells in a food processor until fine. Combine the shells with the butter, garlic, peppercorns, allspice, and bay leaf in a small, heavy saucepan. Bring to a boil, then reduce the heat and simmer, stirring occasionally, for 40 to 45 minutes, or until flavorful. Strain through a cheesecloth-lined fine-mesh sieve. Gather the corners of the cheesecloth together over the shells and wring out any remaining butter.

This butter keeps for several weeks tightly sealed in the refrigerator or several months in the freezer.

LEMON, PARSLEY, AND CAPER BROWN BUTTER
MAKES 8 SERVINGS

This butter, otherwise known as sauce meunière, is usually served over delicate white fish fillets that have been dredged in flour and sautéed, but it is also good with chicken, pork, and veal cutlets and vegetables. The lemon and capers provide the perfect foil to the richness of brown butter. If you store this butter, it's nice to throw in some additional fresh parsley right before serving.

> 8 tablespoons (1 stick) unsalted butter, diced
> 2 tablespoons capers, drained
> 2 tablespoons freshly squeezed lemon juice
> 2 tablespoons minced flat-leaf parsley
> ½ teaspoon kosher salt, or to taste
> Generous pinch of freshly ground black pepper

Heat a small, heavy saucepan over medium heat until very hot. Add the butter and cook, stirring constantly, for 4 to 5 minutes, or until browned. Remove the pan from the heat, add capers, lemon juice, parsley, salt, and pepper, and stir until the bubbling subsides. Serve the butter warm.

This butter keeps for several days tightly sealed in the refrigerator or several weeks in the freezer.

SAGE BROWN BUTTER
MAKES 8 SERVINGS

*T*his aromatic butter is a classic sauce for gnocchi and squash ravioli. Don't be afraid to use whole sage leaves here—when they hit the hot butter, they become crisp like chips and their flavor mellows considerably.

8 tablespoons (1 stick) unsalted butter, diced
¼ cup sage leaves
½ teaspoon kosher salt, or to taste
Generous pinch of freshly ground black pepper

Heat a small, heavy saucepan over medium heat until very hot. Add the butter and cook, stirring constantly, for 4 to 5 minutes, or until browned. Remove the pan from the heat; add the sage, salt, and pepper; and stir until the bubbling subsides. Serve the butter warm.

This butter keeps for several days tightly sealed in the refrigerator or several weeks in the freezer.

Sweet
BUTTERS

Recipes for fruity butters are first up. Butters
flavored with spices, coffee, caramel, and
chocolate round out the chapter.

BED & BREAKFAST BUTTER

MAKES 8 SERVINGS

*T*his butter is served at practically every B&B at breakfast time and for good reason—it's effortless to make and yet somehow makes simple butter and jam seem like a special treat. Fruit preserves of any kind, including jam, jelly, and marmalade, will work here.

Serve with typical breakfast fare: pancakes, waffles, French toast, or crêpes. Or just spread it on toast.

8 tablespoons (1 stick) unsalted butter, softened
¼ cup fruit preserves

Blend together the butter and fruit preserves in a medium-size bowl. Form into a log and refrigerate until firm before slicing and serving, or use another shaping method (see pages 16–17). If you've made the butter with a chunky preserve or marmalade, it won't be suitable for piping, molding, cookie-cutter shapes, or curling.

ORANGE-HONEY BUTTER
MAKES 8 SERVINGS

*H*oney butter is good with a wide variety of breakfast fare. It goes especially well with cornbread and other quick breads made with cornmeal.

    8 tablespoons (1 stick) unsalted butter, softened
    2 tablespoons honey, preferably orange blossom
    1 tablespoon grated orange zest

Blend together the butter, honey, and zest in a medium-size bowl. Form into a log and refrigerate until firm before slicing and serving, or use another shaping method (see pages 16–17).

VARIATION
• *Meyer Lemon–Honey Butter:* Substitute Meyer lemon zest for the orange zest.

"Eat butter first, and eat it last, and live till a hundred years be past."

—Dutch proverb

VERY BERRY BUTTER

MAKES 8 SERVINGS

The character of freeze-dried berries is completely different from that of fresh or conventionally dried ones. They're more like candy than fruit, and their melt-in-your-mouth texture means they blend into butter readily. The result is a vividly colored and flavored butter to slather on any of your favorite breakfast items, from bagels and toast to pancakes and waffles to muffins and scones.

Try freeze-dried strawberries, raspberries, or blackberries, or a combination of all three, for this recipe.

½ ounce freeze-dried berries
8 tablespoons (1 stick) unsalted butter, softened
2 tablespoons confectioners' sugar

Grind the freeze-dried berries to a fine powder in a blender or spice mill. Blend together the berry powder, butter, and confectioners' sugar in a medium-size bowl. Form into a log and refrigerate until firm before slicing and serving, or use another shaping method (see pages 16–17).

ROSE-BERRY BUTTER

MAKES 8 SERVINGS

$\mathcal{U}$se fresh raspberries for this butter in the summertime; go with thawed frozen ones the rest of the year. Adjust the amount of sugar depending on the sweetness of the berries. Using a sieve rather than a food processor to puree the raspberries removes the seeds.

This fragrant butter does double duty as a breakfast spread and as a frosting. For a special way to start the day, top your pancakes, waffles, crêpes, or French toast with a generous pat of this butter, a handful of mixed berries, and a dusting of confectioners' sugar. To ice a two-layer white cake or 24 cupcakes, triple the recipe.

Rose water can be found at Mediterranean and Middle Eastern markets.

> 2 ounces (about ½ cup) raspberries
> 8 tablespoons (1 stick) unsalted butter, softened
> ¼ cup confectioners' sugar
> 1 teaspoon rose water (see Source Guide, page 92)

Force the raspberries through a fine-mesh sieve. Blend together the raspberry puree, butter, confectioners' sugar, and rose water in a medium-size bowl.

To use as a butter, form into a log and refrigerate until firm before slicing and serving, or use another shaping method (see pages 16–17).

To use as a buttercream frosting, let soften if needed and spread onto cooled baked goods, swirling decoratively.

VARIATION

• *Rose-Blackberry Butter:* Substitute blackberries for the raspberries.

APRICOT-ALMOND BUTTER
MAKES 8 SERVINGS

*T*ry this butter at breakfast time and you may forgo the maple syrup.

6 dried apricot halves
8 tablespoons (1 stick) unsalted butter, softened
¼ cup sliced almonds, toasted (see page 12)
2 tablespoons confectioners' sugar
¼ teaspoon vanilla extract

Combine the apricots and enough boiling water to cover in a bowl and let soak for 10 to 12 minutes, or until rehydrated. Transfer the apricots to a paper towel–lined plate and drain for about a minute.

Combine the apricots, butter, almonds, confectioners' sugar, and vanilla in a food processor and pulse until smooth. Form into a log and refrigerate until firm before slicing and serving, pack into ramekins, or simply serve by the dollop (see pages 16–17).

> "Honest bread is very well—it's the butter that makes the temptation."
> —Douglas Jerrold

PASSION FRUIT BUTTER
MAKES 8 SERVINGS

*P*assion fruit may be considered exotic on the mainland, but in Hawaii it's ubiquitous. Hawaiians call it *lilikoi* and use it with great abandon, adding it to everything from cocktails to butter. On a recent trip to Maui, I had French toast with *lilikoi* butter one morning and enjoyed it so much that I had to replicate it when I returned home. I made an island-inspired French toast by substituting coconut milk for the regular milk in my usual recipe, and I used fresh passion fruit in the butter. (Incidentally, this sort of milk substitution also works with pancakes, waffles, and crêpes, any of which would be perfect with this tropical butter.)

When buying passion fruit, look for fruit that's "shrinkled"—that's my word for shrunken and wrinkled, and trust me when I say there's no better way to describe a ripe passion fruit.

1 passion fruit
8 tablespoons (1 stick) unsalted butter, softened
1 tablespoon confectioners' sugar

Halve the passion fruit and scoop out the flesh with a spoon. Blend together the passion fruit flesh, butter, and confectioners' sugar in a medium-size bowl. Form into a log and refrigerate until firm before slicing and serving, or use another shaping method (see pages 16–17).

MAPLE-CINNAMON BUTTER WITH BRANDIED RAISINS

MAKES 8 SERVINGS

*T*his is for times when you want the classic flavor of butter and maple syrup on your pancakes but with just a little twist. It's perfect for brunch. To make it nonalcoholic, substitute apple cider for the brandy.

¼ cup raisins, preferably golden
1 tablespoon brandy
8 tablespoons (1 stick) unsalted butter, softened
2 tablespoons maple syrup
⅛ teaspoon ground cinnamon

Combine the raisins and brandy in a small bowl and let soak, stirring occasionally, for about 2 hours, or until all of the brandy has been absorbed.

Blend together the brandied raisins, butter, syrup, and cinnamon in a medium-size bowl. Form into a log and refrigerate until firm before slicing and serving, pack into ramekins, or simply serve by the dollop (see pages 16–17).

VARIATIONS

• *Maple-Cinnamon Butter with Brandied Sour Cherries:* Substitute dried sour cherries for the raisins.
• *Maple-Cinnamon Butter with Brandied Cranberries:* Substitute dried cranberries for the raisins.

WHIPPED VANILLA BEAN BUTTER
MAKES 8 SERVINGS

*T*op your pancakes, waffles, or toast with this lightly sweetened butter, and you'll feel like you're having dessert for breakfast. Increase the amount of sugar if you like it sweeter. Unsweetened, it can be used for sautéing fruit and in lieu of plain butter in baked goods.

8 tablespoons (1 stick) unsalted butter, softened
1 vanilla bean
1 tablespoon sugar

In a mixer fitted with the paddle attachment, beat the butter on medium speed until light and creamy.

With a paring knife, cut the vanilla bean in half lengthwise. Use the tip of the knife to scrape out the seeds, reserving the pod for another use. Add the vanilla seeds and sugar to the butter and beat until blended, stopping the mixer once or twice to scrape down the sides of the bowl.

To use as a butter, pack into ramekins, pipe, or simply serve by the dollop as described on page 17.

To use as a buttercream frosting, spread onto cooled baked goods, swirling decoratively. Soften and rewhip this butter before using or serving if it's been chilled or frozen.

VARIATIONS
- *Citrus–Vanilla Bean Butter:* Blend in 2 teaspoons grated orange zest and 2 teaspoons grated lemon zest.
- *Lavender–Vanilla Bean Butter:* Grind ½ teaspoon dried lavender flowers using a mortar and pestle and blend into the butter. Make sure you're using culinary lavender, which has not been sprayed with pesticides.

PIE SPICE BUTTER

MAKES 8 SERVINGS

In the fall, whip up a batch of this butter to enjoy slathered on the apple- and pumpkin-flavored baked goods of the season.

8 tablespoons (1 stick) unsalted butter, softened
2 tablespoons confectioners' sugar
1½ teaspoons ground cinnamon
½ teaspoon ground ginger
¼ teaspoon ground cloves
⅛ teaspoon freshly ground nutmeg
½ teaspoon vanilla extract

Blend together the butter, confectioners' sugar, cinnamon, ginger, cloves, nutmeg, and vanilla in a medium-size bowl. Form into a log and refrigerate until firm before slicing and serving, or use another shaping method (see pages 16–17).

COFFEE BUTTER

MAKES 8 SERVINGS

If a cup of coffee with your breakfast just isn't enough, then spread this butter on your toast or scone.

2 tablespoons turbinado sugar
8 tablespoons (1 stick) unsalted butter, softened
1 teaspoon instant espresso powder

Grind the turbinado sugar to a fine powder in a mortar and pestle or a spice mill. Blend together the sugar, butter, and espresso powder in a medium-size bowl. Form into a log and refrigerate until firm before slicing and serving, or use another shaping method (see pages 16–17).

SALTED CARAMEL BUTTER
MAKES 8 SERVINGS

*T*his creamy butter is such a treat that it shouldn't be reserved for the breakfast table. Spread it on vanilla cupcakes or sandwich it between chocolate cookies.

¼ cup sugar
3 tablespoons water
¼ cup heavy cream
8 tablespoons (1 stick) unsalted butter, softened
½ teaspoon *fleur de sel* or other finishing sea salt, or to taste
⅛ teaspoon vanilla extract

Combine the sugar and water in a small, heavy saucepan. Bring to a boil, brush down the sides of the pan with water, and boil until caramelized, 5 to 6 minutes. The sugar will be fragrant and have a deep amber color when it is caramelized. Remove the pan from the heat, slowly stir in the cream until smooth, and let cool to room temperature.

Blend together the caramel, butter, salt, and vanilla in a medium-size bowl.

To use as a butter, form into a log and refrigerate until firm before slicing and serving, or use another shaping method (see pages 16–17).

To use as a buttercream frosting, let soften if needed and spread onto cooled baked goods, swirling decoratively.

VARIATION
• *Caramel-Pecan Butter:* Blend ¼ cup chopped toasted pecans into the butter. This variation is not suitable for piping, molding, cookie-cutter shapes, or curling.

HAZELNUT PRALINE BUTTER
MAKES 8 SERVINGS

If you like your caramel butter to have a bit of a crunch, this one's for you.

¼ **cup sugar**
3 **tablespoons water**
¼ **cup hazelnuts, toasted and skinned (see page 12)**
8 **tablespoons (1 stick) unsalted butter, softened**

Combine the sugar and water in a small, heavy saucepan. Bring to a boil, brush down the sides of the pan with water, and boil until caramelized, 5 to 6 minutes. The sugar will be fragrant and have a deep amber color when it is caramelized. Remove the pan from the heat, stir in the hazelnuts, and pour onto a parchment-lined baking sheet. Let cool to room temperature and break into pieces.

Combine the praline and the butter in a food processor and pulse until smooth. Form into a log and refrigerate until firm before slicing and serving, or use another shaping method (see pages 16–17).

"Butter! Give me butter! Always butter!"
—Fernand Point

WHIPPED CHOCOLATE BUTTER

MAKES 12 SERVINGS, OR ENOUGH FROSTING FOR A 9-INCH
SINGLE-LAYER CAKE OR A DOZEN CUPCAKES

*n*ot only is this an indulgent topping for pancakes, waffles, toast, and muffins, it can also be used as a simple
buttercream for frosting cakes and cupcakes and for filling
sandwich cookies.

5 ounces semisweet chocolate, chopped, or ⅔ cup semisweet
   chocolate chips
12 tablespoons (1½ sticks) unsalted butter, softened
¾ cup confectioners' sugar
½ teaspoon vanilla extract

Melt the chocolate in a small heatproof bowl set over a saucepan of simmering water, stirring frequently. Let cool slightly.

In a mixer fitted with the paddle attachment, beat the butter on medium speed until light and creamy. Add the confectioners' sugar and vanilla and beat until blended. Add the
chocolate and continue to beat until smooth, stopping the
mixer once or twice to scrape down the sides of the bowl.

To use as a butter, pack into ramekins, pipe, or simply serve
by the dollop as described on page 17.

To use as a buttercream frosting, spread onto cooled baked
goods, swirling decoratively. Soften and rewhip this butter
before using or serving if it's been chilled or frozen.

VARIATIONS

• *Mint Chocolate Butter:* Blend in ⅛ teaspoon peppermint extract.
• *Mocha Butter:* Blend in 2 teaspoons instant espresso powder.

HUNGRY CRAVINGS

For more cooking inspiration, information, and the latest news on my culinary adventures, please visit my blog www.hungrycravings.com. There you will find several tutorials demonstrating techniques used for recipes in this book.

How to julienne an onion:
www.hungrycravings.com/2008/09/cutting-onions-slice-versus-julienne.html

How to mince a shallot:
www.hungrycravings.com/2008/12/shallot-minced.html

How to roast a bell pepper:
www.hungrycravings.com/2009/01/roasted-peppers-chiles.html

SOURCE GUIDE

Dean & Deluca
www.deandeluca.com
Specialty groceries, including ancho chile powder, black sesame seeds, caviar, *fleur de sel*, foie gras, *herbes de Provence*, lavender, pasilla chile powder, smoked salt, Spanish paprika, truffle salt, vanilla beans, vanilla extract, and white peppercorns.

Penzeys Spices
www.penzeys.com
Dry herbs and spices, including black sesame seeds, lavender, saffron, Spanish paprika, vanilla beans, vanilla extract, and white peppercorns.

The Spanish Table
www.spanishtable.com
Spanish foods, including saffron and Spanish paprika.

The Tao of Tea
www.taooftea.com
Matcha tea.

Trader Joe's
www.traderjoes.com
Groceries, including freeze-dried berries.

Sur La Table
www.surlatable.com
Cooks' tools and equipment, including Microplanes and parchment paper sheets.

Whole Foods Market
www.wholefoodsmarket.com
High-quality groceries, including ancho chiles, black sesame seeds, canned chipotles in adobo, cultured butter, dried porcini mushrooms, dried shiitake mushrooms, fresh herbs, goat's milk butter, Gorgonzola, guajillo chiles, *herbes de Provence*, kimchi, kosher salt, lavender, matcha tea, miso, Parmigiano-Reggiano, pasilla chiles, rose water, ruby port, saffron, smoked salt, Spanish paprika, toasted sesame oil, vanilla beans, vanilla extract, and wasabi powder.

MEASUREMENT EQUIVALENTS

LIQUID CONVERSIONS

US	Metric
1 tsp	5 ml
1 tbs	15 ml
2 tbs	30 ml
3 tbs	45 ml
¼ cup	60 ml
⅓ cup	75 ml
⅓ cup + 1 tbs	90 ml
⅓ cup + 2 tbs	100 ml
½ cup	120 ml
⅔ cup	150 ml
¾ cup	180 ml
¾ cup + 2 tbs	200 ml
1 cup	240 ml
1 cup + 2 tbs	275 ml
1¼ cups	300 ml
1⅓ cups	325 ml
1½ cups	350 ml
1⅔ cups	375 ml
1¾ cups	400 ml
1¾ cups + 2 tbs	450 ml
2 cups (1 pint)	475 ml
2½ cups	600 ml
3 cups	720 ml
4 cups (1 quart)	945 ml

(1,000 ml is 1 liter)

NOTE: All conversions are approximate.

WEIGHT CONVERSIONS

US/UK	Metric
½ oz	14 g
1 oz	28 g
1½ oz	43 g
2 oz	57 g
2½ oz	71 g
3 oz	85 g
3½ oz	100 g
4 oz	113 g
5 oz	142 g
6 oz	170 g
7 oz	200 g
8 oz	227 g
9 oz	255 g
10 oz	284 g
11 oz	312 g
12 oz	340 g
13 oz	368 g
14 oz	400 g
15 oz	425 g
1 lb	454 g

OVEN TEMPERATURE CONVERSIONS

°F	Gas Mark	°C
250	½	120
275	1	140
300	2	150
325	3	165
350	4	180
375	5	190
400	6	200
425	7	220
450	8	230
475	9	240
500	10	260
550	Broil	290

INDEX

ACKNOWLEDGMENTS

Thank you to Bruce Shaw, Adam Salomone, and Dan Rosenberg of The Harvard Common Press for imagining this book and then giving me the chance to write it.

Thanks to my husband for being my tireless taste tester, proofreader, and cheerleader.

And thanks to my little brother, Andrew, for being my sounding board.

ABOUT THE AUTHOR

LUCY VASERFIRER is a chef, culinary educator, blogger, and cookbook author. Her first book was *Seared to Perfection: The Simple Art of Sealing in Flavor*, which Marie Simmons called "masterful yet practical" and Janie Hibler said is "a must for any serious home cook." Her blog, Hungry Cravings, demystifies complicated cooking and baking techniques and offers delicious, foolproof recipes. Lucy teaches at Clark College in Washington and Mount Hood Community College in Oregon and has taught both home and professional cooks and bakers for years. A Le Cordon Bleu graduate, she lives with her husband in Vancouver, Washington.